TONGUE-TIED TING TING

TEXT BY FELIX CHEONG
ILLUSTRATED BY ISAAC LIANG

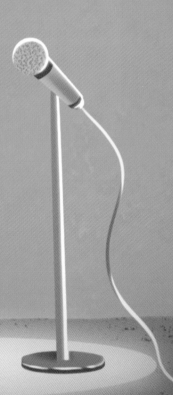

mc Marshall Cavendish
Children

When Ting Ting sings,

BINS

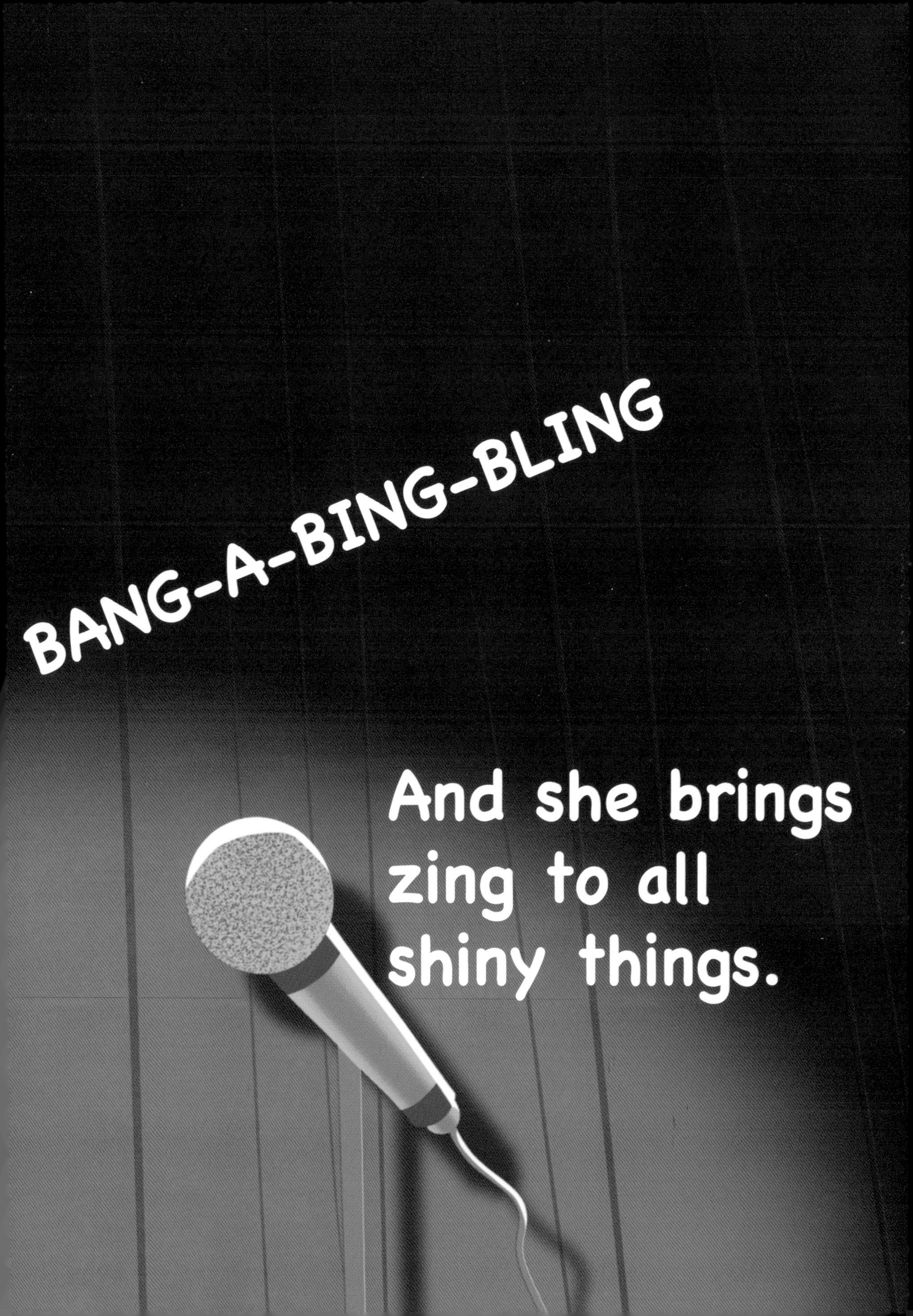

BANG-A-BING-BLING

And she brings
zing to all
shiny things.

Ying Ying, her twin, sings too
but not too distinct
As when Ting Ting sings
to her own instinct.

Tweens do not twitch a bit
or itch an inch.

When her pitch hits high
reach and bewitch rich.

"Born for song, I long to belong.
In movies that move me in story and song.

I am among stars that shine sure and bright,
my words will move you with their music and light.

One's wants may well wear wane and wan,
But not my songs that unknot the tongue!"

But when Ting Ting speaks, nothing seeps,
Not a squeak leaks from her voice box deep.

Try as she might, by daylight or bright night,
Her words nigh fly high but fight shy to stay dry.

She points,

and she writes.

She blinks,

She frowns,

She laughs,

and she cries.

But she makes no sentence that makes sense.
Her family contends she must be dense.

Dad thinks that Ting Ting says nothing.
Because she cannot match her twin Ying Ying,

Who thought up tall tales told thrice at two,
While Ting Ting sang and was all she could do.

They might dress and look alike in all nooks,
But by crook or by hook, what they would not brook!

"Let her keep mum," Mum keeps her sigh light.
"When she gets it, she will get it right."

One day, Ting Ting overhears Ying Ying trying to shh, sha, shoo, shay, say something.

Meanwhile Ting Ting smiles a mile-wide smile
And starts to sing in her sweet, smooth style:

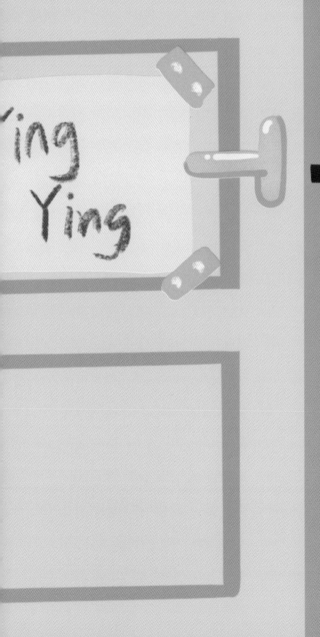

"She sells seashells by the seashore.
The shells she sells are surely seashells.

So if she sells shells on the seashore,
I am sure she sells seashore shells."

Ying Ying stares at her sister in surprise.
How effortless she makes it at first try!

"Slow down. I cannot keep up with the tune."

Ting Ting does, one word at a time, and soon.

The twins are entwined in tune. Slowly,
Ting Ting is speaking, shyly, surely.

She hears her own voice able to talk and tell
Like a new world in a seashore seashell.

About the Writer

Felix Cheong is the award-winning author of 19 books. Named Young Artist of the Year by the National Arts Council in 2000, he is currently a university lecturer. *Tongue-Tied Ting Ting* is his sixth children's picture book. For more on his works, visit www.felixcheong.net

About the Illustrator

Isaac Liang is a deaf illustrator who started his artistic
journey at the age of four by drawing on cupboards
with crayons. In his free time, he gains inspiration from
traveling and café-hopping. Through his illustrations,
animations, and traditional art mediums, Isaac amplifies
visions and tell visual stories in a unique way. For more
info, visit www.isaacliang.com

Published by Marshall Cavendish Children
An imprint of Marshall Cavendish International

A member of the
Times Publishing Group

Other Marshall Cavendish Offices:
Marshall Cavendish Corporation, 800 Westchester Ave, Suite N-641, Rye Brook, NY 10573, USA •
Marshall Cavendish International (Thailand) Co Ltd, 253 Asoke, 16th Floor, Sukhumvit 21 Road,
Klongtoey Nua, Wattana, Bangkok 10110, Thailand • Marshall Cavendish (Malaysia) Sdn Bhd,
Times Subang, Lot 46, Subang Hi-Tech Industrial Park, Batu Tiga, 40000 Shah Alam, Selangor
Darul Ehsan, Malaysia

National Library Board, Singapore Cataloguing in Publication Data

Name(s): Cheong, Felix. | Liang, Isaac, illustrator.
Title: Tongue-tied Ting Ting / text by Felix Cheong ; illustrated by Isaac Liang.
Description: Singapore : Marshall Cavendish Children, [2021]
Identifier(s): OCN 1251849856 | ISBN 978-981-4974-41-7 (hardcover)
Subject(s): LCSH: Tongue twisters--Juvenile fiction. | Stories in rhyme.
Classification: DDC 428.6--dc23

Printed in Singapore